The Oxford Piano Method

PIANO TIME JAZZ

Book 1

T0056977

Pauline Hall

MUSIC DEPARTMENT

OXFORD
UNIVERSITY PRESS

OXFORD
UNIVERSITY PRESS

Great Clarendon Street, Oxford OX2 6DP, England
198 Madison Avenue, New York, NY10016, USA

Oxford University Press is a department of the University of Oxford.
It furthers the University's aim of excellence in research, scholarship,
and education by publishing worldwide in

Oxford New York
Auckland Cape Town Hong Kong Karachi
Kuala Lumpur Madrid Melbourne Mexico City Nairobi
New Delhi Shanghai Taipei Toronto

With offices in

Argentina Austria Brazil Chile Czech Republic France Greece
Guatemala Hungary Italy Japan Poland Portugal Singapore
South Korea Switzerland Thailand Turkey Ukraine Vietnam

Oxford is a registered trade mark of Oxford University Press
in the UK and in certain other countries

© Oxford University Press 1999

Pauline Hall has asserted her right under the Copyright, Designs
and Patents Act, 1988, to be identified as the Author of this Work

Database right Oxford University Press (maker)

First published 1999

All rights reserved. No part of this publication may be reproduced,
stored in a retrieval system, or transmitted, in any form or by any means,
without the prior permission in writing of Oxford University Press,
or as expressly permitted by law. Enquiries concerning reproduction
outside the scope of the above should be sent to the Music Copyright
Department, Oxford University Press, at the address above

Permission to perform the works in this anthology in public
(except in the course of divine worship) should normally be obtained
from the Performing Right Society Ltd. (PRS), 29/33 Berners Street,
London W1T 3AB, or its affiliated Societies in each country throughout
the world, unless the owner or the occupier of the premises
being used holds a licence from the Society

Permission to make a recording must be obtained in advance
from the Mechanical-Copyright Protection Society Ltd. (MCPS),
Elgar House, 41 Streatham High Road, London SW16 1ER,
or its affiliated Societies in each country throughout the world

32

ISBN 978-0-19-372733-5

Illustrations by Andy Hammond

Music and text origination by
Barnes Music Engraving Ltd., East Sussex
Printed in Great Britain on acid-free paper by
Halstan & Co. Ltd., Amersham, Bucks.

Contents

Tick tock boogie	4
Driving force	5
Saturday stroll	6
Hop, skip and jump	7
Cheeky Charlie	8
The sloop 'John B'	9
Tango for starters	10
Cowboy blues	11
Marching in again	12
Tea for one cha-cha	13
Brown jug boogie	14
Temper tantrum tango	15
Friday night rag	16
Hey, Lawdy!	17
Lollipop rock	18
Coconut calypso	19
Living it up	20
City express	21
Come on and boogie	22
Window shopping	23
Homework blues	24
Mexican fiesta	25
A story book romance	26
Bus stop blues	27
Got a new car!	28
Creepy crawly	29
Somewhere that's sunny	30
Sherbet fizz	31
Street parade	32

Tick tock boogie

FIONA MACARDLE

Driving force

FIONA MACARDLE

Saturday stroll

DAVID BLACKWELL

Hop, skip and jump

FIONA MACARDLE

Cheeky Charlie

FIONA MACARDLE

The sloop 'John B'

PAULINE HALL

The wreck of the sailing ship 'John B' lies at the bottom of Nassau harbour.

Tango for starters

FIONA MACARDLE

Cowboy blues

PAULINE HALL

Marching in again

FIONA MACARDLE

Tea for one cha-cha

STEPHEN DURO

Brown jug boogie

PAULINE HALL

Temper tantrum tango

FIONA MACARDLE

Really feel as though you want to go to your bedroom and bang the door!

Friday night rag

ALAN BULLARD

Hey, Lawdy!

STEPHEN DURO

Lollipop rock

PAULINE HALL

Coconut calypso

PAULINE HALL

Living it up

ALAN BULLARD

City express

DAVID BLACKWELL

Come on and boogie

RODERICK SKEAPING

Window shopping

PAUL DRAYTON

Homework blues

FIONA MACARDLE

Mexican fiesta

PAULINE HALL

A story book romance

STEPHEN DURO

Bus stop blues

PAULINE HALL

Got a new car!

RODERICK SKEAPING

Got a new car! and I'm just goin' to get it, 'cos it's Tues-day to - day!
Creepy crawly
PETER GRITTON
Sinister

Somewhere that's sunny

RODERICK SKEAPING

Sherbet fizz

FIONA MACARDLE

Street parade

PAUL DRAYTON